BRANIFF AIRWAYS
FLYING COLORS

Pictured here is a Braniff International Boeing 747 on final approach at Dallas/Forth Worth Regional (now International) Airport (DFW) in 1979. (Courtesy of Braniff Flying Colors Collection/History of Aviation Collection.)

On the Front Cover: Braniff International Boeing 747-127 registered as N601BN, dubbed *747 Braniff Place*, is taxiing at Dallas/Fort Worth Regional Airport in 1979. The famous bright orange jumbo jet was the flagship of Braniff's fleet from 1971 until 1982. (Courtesy of Braniff Flying Colors Collection/History of Aviation Collection.)

On the Back Cover: At left, Braniff International Airways Douglas DC-6 registered as N90885 is parked at Dallas Love Field in the early 1950s. The four-engine airliner joined the fleet in 1947, and was assigned to domestic and Latin America service. At center, Braniff flight attendants are modeling new Classic Collection uniforms on the airside ramp at the Dallas Love Field base in 1974. Introduced that year, this was Emilio Pucci's final full collection for Braniff International. At right, Braniff International president Harding L. Lawrence is standing near Braniff's first new Boeing 727 Trijet airliner in May 1966. Lawrence joined the airline in April 1965, after a highly successful 10-year tenure at Continental Airlines, where he presided over 500 percent growth of the airline. (All, courtesy of Braniff Flying Colors Collection/History of Aviation Collection.)

BRANIFF AIRWAYS
FLYING COLORS

Richard Benjamin Cass

ARCADIA
PUBLISHING

Published by Arcadia Publishing
Charleston, South Carolina

Printed in the United States of America

Library of Congress Control Number: 2015937177

For all general information, please contact Arcadia Publishing:
Telephone 843-853-2070
Fax 843-853-0044
E-mail sales@arcadiapublishing.com
For customer service and orders:
Toll-Free 1-888-313-2665

Visit us on the Internet at www.arcadiapublishing.com

Dedicated to the memory of Harding Luther Lawrence:
"Braniff is my vocation and my avocation."

CONTENTS

ACKNOWLEDGMENTS

The former employees of Braniff Airways are known collectively as the Braniff family simply because even after the original airline, which has not existed in over three decades, the tenacity and love for their beloved company remains as strong as it ever was. It was this bravado and can-do attitude of Braniff's employees that propelled it to set so many industry records. I want to thank each of these fine people for him or her giving a seven-year-old the opportunity to know and admire their company and for today sharing with me their personal recollections of the day-to-day operations at Braniff.

This book would not have been possible without the unending support of my friends at the University of Texas at Dallas History of Aviation Collection at McDermott Library, which houses the Braniff Airways Public Relations Archive. Half of the photographs in this book are attributed to the History of Aviation Collection's (HAC) remarkable collection of Braniff's history, immaculately maintained by director Paul A. Oelkrug, curator Dr. Thomas Allen, and curator Patrizia Nava.

The remainder of the materials and photographs in this book are derived from my personal Braniff Flying Colors (BFC) collection. My collection of Braniff began when I was seven years old and has been a lifelong endeavor that I dearly love and enjoy. This book, in many ways, represents my five decades of collecting Braniff.

INTRODUCTION

Two brothers, a dreamer and a pragmatist, joined forces to create one of the world's leading airlines, Braniff Airways. From humble beginnings as an aero club in Oklahoma City in 1927, Braniff grew to become a multinational corporation that flew throughout the continental United States, Canada, and Mexico, from the US mainland to South America, and across both the Pacific and the Atlantic Oceans. Those brothers, Paul Revere Braniff, the dreamer and aviator, and Thomas Elmer Braniff, the pragmatist who had already created a burgeoning insurance empire, had the courage and foresight to become early pioneers in America's fledgling aviation industry.

Their first operating venture, Paul R. Braniff, Inc., formed in the spring of 1928, took to the air on its maiden flight on June 20, 1928, with a five-passenger single-engine Stinson Detroiter. The new airline flew oil-company executives between Oklahoma City, Oklahoma, where Braniff was based, to Tulsa, Oklahoma, the heart of the Oklahoma oil boom. The airline was completely dependent on passenger fares for its existence. A large aviation holding company that was hoping to build an air and rail network from coast to coast purchased Paul R. Braniff, Inc., in 1929, and in 1930 the company was absorbed by the predecessor of American Airlines.

The brothers, now with aviation in their blood, once again joined together to create the airline company that would eventually span the globe, Braniff Airways, Inc., in November 1930. Once again, the new company was dependent on passenger fares for its continued operation, and with the country in the throes of the Great Depression, finding passengers with money to fill their Lockheed Vega aircraft was not a small task. The airline was close to collapse when in 1934 it was awarded its first airmail contract between Chicago and Oklahoma City. Government corruption brought a saving grace to Braniff and the rest of the fledgling airlines that traversed the United States. Braniff Airways now had the support of not only passenger fares but also guaranteed airmail payments that virtually guaranteed its existence.

The company began a steady growth while becoming the surviving carrier after merging with two small airlines that further increased the size of its route system while strengthening its airmail payments by adding new postal routes. By 1940, the carrier had upgraded to the ubiquitous 21-passenger Douglas DC-3 twin-engine airliner that revolutionized the entire airline industry and overnight made it a safe and reliable method of transportation. By the summer of 1942, the airline moved its headquarters to Dallas Love Field, which had become the central terminus of its core operations and linked the Great Lakes to Texas. Braniff's growth, along with the rest of the industry, was slowed by the global war, which required the assets of nearly every company in the United States, and that specifically included the troop-carrying capacity of passenger aircraft.

After World War II, Braniff's fortunes would only explode, with the company receiving approval to operate between the US mainland and Central America, Cuba, and deep into the South American continent. Large four-engine Douglas DC-4 and DC-6 airliners were added to the fleet and specifically purchased for operation over the company's 7,000-mile route system south of the border. International script was added to the corporate masthead in 1946. Service began from Dallas to Cuba, Central America, and South America on June 4, 1948, and with that, little Braniff Airways became an international airline of sizable measure. Strangely, Braniff would not be authorized to serve Mexico until the 1960s, although Tom Braniff had operated a small Mexican airline, Aerovias Braniff, during 1945. Because of intergovernmental disagreements stemming from Aerovias Braniff, Braniff Airways was denied the chance to link the United States with its closest neighbor to the south.

Braniff continued to expand its South American route system into the early 1950s, but costs caused the need for greater subsidy to ensure the airline was not losing money, which could affect its domestic operations. The Latin American division, or LAD, did not officially make a cent until 1965. The airline grew again by merger with a small Midwestern carrier, Mid-Continent Airlines, based in Kansas City, in August 1952. The untimely loss of Braniff's president, Tom Braniff, in a private plane crash in January 1954 saw the first change in management since 1935, when Paul Braniff left the company to pursue other ventures. An able manager, Charles Edmund Beard was hired as his replacement, with Beard assuming most of Paul's duties. It was Charles Beard who stepped forward to graciously accept the helm in January 1954, now that the company's cherished cofounder was gone.

Beard successfully flew Braniff into the jet-powered age in 1959 with the introduction of the Lockheed L-188 Electra four-engine turboprop followed by the pure jet Boeing 707 in December of that year. The airline had expanded operations across the eastern United States to Newark, New Jersey, and Washington, DC, and via an interchange with Eastern Airlines through Miami, Florida, which served as another gateway to feed the company's South America system. Earlier in the 1950s, Beard had proposed merging Braniff with Pan American Grace Airways, the largest US airline operating in South America, but resistance by the airline's half owner Pan American had scuttled the merger until 1967.

After the death of Tom Braniff, followed by his wife, Bess, in August 1954, the ownership of the airline was left to the Blakley/Braniff Foundation. In the early 1960s, the company was sold to a group of Texas Instruments executives, and in 1964 it was sold again to Greatamerica Insurance Company. The executives of Greatamercia had identified Braniff as a well-run and stable company but a highly underutilized operation that could, with an overhaul, become a world-class airline that might span the globe. The Greatamerica management was correct, and in less than two years Braniff became the talk of the town and assumed the throne as the king of promotion.

Charles Beard announced his intention to retire from Braniff in November 1964, and a search commenced for a new chief. A leader and a maverick was found in a young Continental Airlines executive vice president, Harding Luther Lawrence, who was responsible for mastering 500 percent growth at the small trunk airline in the 10 years he was with the enterprise, all the while being tutored by the magnificent Robert F. Six. At 44 years of age, Lawrence was one of the youngest airline chief executive officers in the country. He began looking over the Braniff operation in February 1965 by visiting every area of the company while taking extensive notes. He was ready to reform Braniff in April 1965, when he assumed the presidency.

Lawrence demanded that a new promotion and advertising program be designed to catapult Braniff into the world spotlight in a very short period of time. To help with this, he hired the New York advertising think tank Jack Tinker and Partners, employer of Mary Wells, who had made a name for herself on Madison Avenue. Wells created a campaign that revolutionized the entire way that airlines presented themselves to the public. The End of the Plain Plane Campaign introduced the airline world to Alexander Girard, who designed over 17,000 public contact items and Emilio Pucci, who designed a space age–themed uniform for ground and flight personnel. Girard designed an amazing palette of bright and vibrant colors that were painted on Braniff's jet aircraft along with corresponding interiors with bright and colorful seat fabrics. Flying on Braniff was stylish and exciting, and the rest of the industry followed.

The public took notice and applauded Braniff's end to the military-themed presentations that had been an airline hallmark since their founding. With this, Braniff began a nonstop period of record growth in traffic and profits for the next 14 years. The company began flying to Hawaii in 1969, which caused the need for a new Boeing 747 that was delivered in January 1971 and painted bright orange. It became the flagship of the fleet and would fly the airline's inaugural flight to London in 1978, the airline's 50th anniversary year, after a two-decade fight to win the authority to fly across the Atlantic Ocean. Alexander Calder was hired in 1972 to paint a full-sized Douglas DC-8, which became the world's first flying canvas, and he repeated the performance again for America's bicentennial in 1976. New, vibrant color schemes were added during the 1970s, and Halston designed an amazing line of easy-to-wear ground- and flight-personnel uniforms.

The Airline Deregulation Act was signed into law in the fall of 1978, and few airlines had any strategy for competing in a nonregulated environment except for Braniff. The company's management felt that the only way for Braniff to survive was to grow and become strong, because in the end, only a small number of large legacy carriers would survive. Braniff took immediate advantage of the new world by adding additional routes and cities as well as aircraft to meet the demands. Many of the international routes that Braniff had applied for as far back as 10 years earlier were now being awarded, and the company began expanding its European service in the summer of 1979. By the fall of that year, the new orange 747s were crossing the Pacific, linking Asia with South America.

Harding Lawrence had transformed Braniff once again and was being hailed as the last airline maverick. A new color scheme adopted in 1978 featured deep, dark, and elegant solid colors with warm light-brown leather interiors. The new look embodied the maturing of Braniff International into a truly world-class airline. However, the global and domestic economic conditions exacerbated by foreign oil markets would not allow Braniff to enjoy its newfound prominence. Virtually as Braniff began its well-planned expansion, unrest in Iran created a crisis that caused oil prices to explode to unprecedented levels from 1979 through 1981. Changes in the Federal Reserve's monetary policy in 1979 caused interest rates to rise to double-digit levels just as Braniff's sparkling new Boeing 727s and Boeing 747s were rolling off the line to meet the demands of the company's impressive route system. Braniff was flying into a storm that no one in the industry believed could ever happen.

Braniff survived for another two years after Harding Lawrence retired in December 1980. In early 1980, he began an immediate program to turn the airline around, which called for reducing capacity by selling unneeded older aircraft and eliminating routes that were now unprofitable because of the prevailing economic conditions. The plan was working, and Braniff was poised to ride out the downturn by 1981 or sooner. Braniff continued to be fraught with unbelievable circumstances arising from the beginning of a severe US recession that began in the summer of 1981, followed by a devastating strike of the nation's air-traffic controllers. Decisions were being made at the company's sleek corporate headquarters on the west side of DFW Airport that led to the company's eventual end in May 1982.

Braniff would fly again in March 1984, but with a return to the military-style presentation that it had fought so hard to shed. In spite of the loss of the industry's high-flying darling, the legend of Braniff continues forward today because of its deep associations with the art, fashion, and design industries. It is because Braniff brought together the mystery and intrigue of aviation with these exciting industries that the airline is still in the public conscience today and will always be remembered and admired by future generations.

Paul Braniff, pictured below in 1929, was the guiding force in enticing his brother Tom Braniff, seen at left in 1920, into joining him to form the first Braniff aviation entity. Paul formed Braniff Air Lines, Inc., on April 26, 1926, but it would not be the first airline to begin operations bearing his name. Paul was born August 30, 1897, in Kansas City and Tom in Salina, Kansas, on December 6, 1883. Tom was the eldest of four children and joined his father, John Braniff, in the insurance business in the early 1900s. Tom eventually opened his own agency, which ultimately financed the brother's aviation ventures. Paul joined the Army and obtained his pilot's license in 1917. He joined Tom in selling insurance, but his love for aviation did not wane. In 1924, he bought his first airplane. (Both, BFC/HAC.)

One

Two Brothers, Paul and Tom

Thomas Elmer Braniff was an insurance magnate by the time he cofounded the Oklahoma Aero Club with his younger brother and pilot Paul Revere Braniff. Paul had fallen in love with the new world of aviation, while Tom was the pragmatic and cautious businessman. However, Paul's love of aviation was transferred to his brother, and as a result, Tom paid off a small Stinson Detroiter five-passenger aircraft that Paul owed money on.

Paul, Tom, and Tom's insurance client E.E. Westervelt of the Bell Telephone Company formed Oklahoma Aero Club to provide an aircraft for executives. As is often the case with group usage of a single item, scheduling problems erupted, and the group disbanded.

Paul and Tom Braniff purchased the remaining interests in the Stinson Detroiter. In May 1928, the men founded Paul R. Braniff, Inc., with the Detroiter, and scheduled service began between Oklahoma City and Tulsa on June 20, 1928.

On November 3, 1930, Braniff Airways, Inc., was formed with Tom Braniff as president, Paul Braniff, secretary and treasurer, and Westervelt as vice president. The airline used single-engine Lockheed Vegas followed by Lockheed L-10 Electra aircraft in 1934, the same year Braniff was awarded its first airmail contracts. Douglas DC-2s, seating 14 passengers, were added in 1937, followed by 21-passenger DC-3s in 1939.

By 1942, Braniff had merged with two smaller Texas carriers and moved all of its operations to Dallas. In 1945, the airline began flying the 52-passenger Douglas DC-4 four-engine airliner and soon ordered the larger DC-6. The airline's fortunes changed precipitously in May 1946, when the carrier was authorized to fly between the mainland United States and Latin America over a 7,719-mile route system. Braniff had become a major airline in less than 20 years.

The Stinson SM-1, Braniff's First Plane. Painted Especially for Capt. Len Morgan

To Len Morgan — one of aviation's great friends. With sincere admiration — Bob Carlin

Travel by Air

Speed   Safety

105 MILES PER HOUR   GOVERNMENT LICENSED SHIPS AND PILOTS

CLOSED CABIN COMFORT
Paul R. Braniff, Operator

TULSA-OKLAHOMA CITY AIRLINE

LEAVE OKLA CITY - 7:00 am-12:00 noon-4:30 p.m.
LEAVE TULSA - 8:30 am-1:30 p.m-6:00 p.m.

$12.50 ONE WAY ~ $20.00 ROUND TRIP

Get all reservations and informations
on Okmulgee-Ponca City Line, from
Hotel or Call ~
YELLOW CAB CO.

In 1927, the brothers formed Oklahoma Aero Club with a group of businessmen. They owned one aircraft for joint use, which became the first Braniff aviation venture. On May 29, 1928, the brothers formed Paul R. Braniff, Inc., with this Stinson Detroiter five-passenger plane, which flew 116 miles between Tulsa and Oklahoma City. In 1990, Braniff captain Len Morgan had the only photograph of Braniff's second Stinson analyzed by Kodak, which determined the color to be maroon. (BFC/HAC.)

Braniff began service on June 20, 1928, with one round-trip flight between Oklahoma City and Tulsa, with Paul piloting the inaugural flight. Paul detailed his first flight during an interview in January 1954 and stated that one passenger was aboard to Tulsa. The company reported a profit after the first 30 days of operation. (BFC/HAC.)

The new Braniff served as a flight school and parts and Travelair dealer for Oklahoma. This Travelair NX6239 was used by Braniff, dubbed the "Tulsa–Oklahoma City Airline," to fly *Daily Oklahoman* newspapers to rural communities. By the end of 1928, Braniff employed 16, including six pilots, flew six airplanes, and had flown 3,000 passengers. Service was extended to Wichita Falls, Texas, with stops at Duncan and Chickasha, Oklahoma. (BFC/HAC.)

In April 1929, the brothers sold the airline to Universal, a large conglomerate of railways and airlines that operated from coast to coast. The new division of Universal was called Braniff Air Lines, Inc., and it extended service to San Angelo and Dallas by midsummer 1929 and then to Amarillo, Texas. Passengers were given a souvenir of their flight that included a biography of their pilot. (BFC/HAC.)

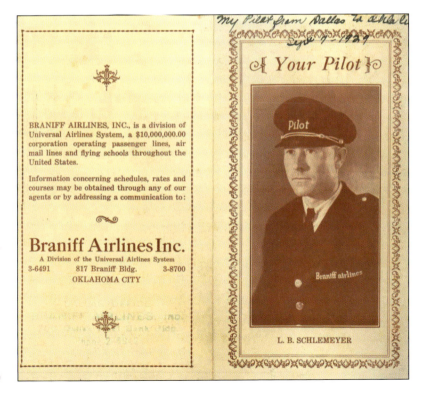

Universal was sold to the Aviation Corporation of New York during the summer of 1929, with all Universal divisions becoming a part of American Airways, the predecessor to American Airlines. Braniff offered many services beyond its passenger and flight-school operations such as air cargo, express, and air ambulance, which were offered in a Travel Air. (BFC/HAC.)

Paul Braniff went to work for a small airline in Mexico before returning to Oklahoma City to form Braniff Airways, Inc., on November 3, 1930. The new airline began operating on November 13 between Oklahoma City and Tulsa and Wichita Falls, with a six-passenger Lockheed Vega aircraft. Ship NC106W, the first Braniff plane equipped with a radio receiver, is parked on the ramp at Oklahoma SW Twenty-Ninth Street Airport in 1935. (BFC/HAC.)

R.V. Carleton was hired as a Vega pilot in June 1931 and became executive vice president of Braniff International in 1964. Braniff's Vegas could fly at 150 miles per hour, and the company advertised as the "World's Fastest Airline," flying only passengers and express packages. Service was expanded from Tulsa to Kansas City on December 5, 1930, and by the end of the year, Braniff employed six and extended service to Chicago in February 1931. (BFC/HAC.)

One of Braniff Airways' first pilots was Ray Carroll Shrader, who commanded the company's first airmail fight in 1934. Captain Shrader, pictured here greeting a passenger at Dallas, became vice president of operations and was the longest-serving Braniff employee at his retirement. Service from St. Louis to Tulsa, Chicago, and Kansas City was added on June 15, 1931. (BFC/HAC.)

By 1933, Braniff's fortunes changed, and the company began to lose money. The Braniff brothers lobbied Congress and on May 7, 1934, received their first airmail contract, AM-9, from Chicago to Dallas. Service was inaugurated on May 17, 1934, and the number of employees grew to 47 in early 1934. Maintenance was moved to Dallas Love Field on November 27. Tom Braniff (second from left) is pictured here with the inaugural Vega NC7953 with Paul Braniff (third from left) and Paul's wife, Marie. (BFC/HAC.)

In January 1935, Braniff merged with Dallas-based Long and Harman Airlines, which operated AM-15 from Dallas to Amarillo, Brownsville, and Galveston, and route miles increased by 1,125. In March 1935, Braniff received its first twin-engine airliner, the Lockheed L-10 Electra, like the one pictured here at the Oklahoma City Air Terminal. (BFC/HAC.)

At the far right, Capt. R.V. Carleton (left) and Capt. Ray Carroll Shrader are on hand for the Electra inaugural from Dallas to Corpus Christi. Sack lunches were served by the copilot aboard the new Electra beginning in September, which marked the first in-flight service on any Braniff aircraft. (BFC/HAC.)

Paul Braniff left the company in 1935 and was replaced by Charles Beard (right), pictured here conducting the first company sales meeting at 10,000 feet aboard a new DC-3 in 1939. Beard rose to the presidency in January 1954. Braniff purchased Fort Worth–based Bowen Airlines in January 1936. The company possessed no airmail contracts but operated "from the Great Lakes to the Gulf," which became Braniff's new slogan. (BFC/HAC.)

Braniff purchased seven Douglas DC-2 twins from Trans World Airlines (TWA) during 1937 and 1938. The luxurious aircraft featured full in-flight meal service and required hostesses. Rebecca Garza and six other girls hired were the first B Line hostesses. Inauguration of DC-2 service began on June 12, 1937, between Dallas and Brownsville. (BFC/HAC.)

The new DC-2 was a revolution for Braniff, allowing the carrier to offer the finest in accommodations for passengers. Luxuriously tailored interiors served to create an elegant atmosphere in tandem with Braniff's new in-flight hostess service. (BFC/HAC.)

Braniff's first hostess uniform was dubbed Bolero and featured a Spanish theme. Designed by Dallas-based Neiman Marcus, the jacket and midi skirt were made of wool worsted in a silver-gray tone. The high-necked jersey blouse was of white silk and complemented with a red sash and red wool crepe turban. (BFC/HAC.)

The Lockheed Vega flew its last flight between Dallas and Amarillo on June 1, 1937. A special farewell ceremony was held at Love Field, featuring a lineup of all three Braniff aircraft. A year later, Braniff celebrated its 10th anniversary and ascension from a 116-mile carrier serving two cities to a 2,963-mile system, flying 8,700 miles daily to 15 cities. (BFC/HAC.)

On August 29, 1939, Tom Braniff announced the purchase of four Douglas DC-3 21-passenger aircraft dubbed the Giant Ship. The first DC-3 NC21773 arrived at Oklahoma City on December 17, 1939, and entered service between Dallas and Amarillo on February 3, 1940. NC21775 was the third DC-3 delivered to Braniff. (BFC/HAC.)

The DC-3 interior was spacious, with reclining seats featuring elegant finishes and expensive fabrics. Tom's daughter, Jeanne Braniff, designed the interiors, which included impressive bulkhead murals that incorporated scenes from Braniff destinations. The DC-3s were dubbed Super B Liners and served until April 1960. By mid-1940, Braniff employed 565, including 79 pilots. (BFC/HAC.)

In October 1940, Braniff moved into the new Lemmon Avenue Terminal from the Love Field Drive Terminal. A new operations base, located where the current terminal is today, opened on November 11, 1941. Braniff's administration offices moved to the new Roanoke Drive "Red Brick Building" by April 1, 1942, making Braniff a Dallas-based carrier. (BFC/HAC.)

Braniff entered the war effort with operation of a cargo route between the continental United States and Panama. The flights, dubbed Banana Run, connected Army depots and bases from San Antonio to the Canal Zone. Braniff's exemplary service played a crucial role in the 1946 route award to Latin America. Braniff's fleet of aircraft was reduced from 16 to seven during the war. (BFC/HAC.)

A Braniff DC-3 is parked at the new Dallas base in 1945. New service inaugurated between 1940 and 1945 included Oklahoma City to Amarillo; Dallas nonstop to Kansas City; Amarillo, Pueblo, and Colorado Springs to Denver; Oklahoma City to Memphis; Topeka was added in 1944, and Lubbock. In spite of wartime, Braniff grew to 3,108 route miles and applied for routes to Latin America in 1943. (BFC/HAC.)

In 1943, Tom Braniff formed Aerovias Braniff to operate throughout Mexico. It was hoped if the airline was established that the Civil Aeronautics Board (CAB) would approve it to become part of Braniff, allowing the company to link Mexico with South America. Service began in the spring of 1945 between Ciudad Laredo and Mexico City. Pan Am pressured the Mexican government, resulting in revocation of Braniff's certificates in October 1946. (BFC/HAC.)

With the conclusion of World War II, Braniff was poised to grow, and five 56-passenger Douglas DC-4 aircraft were ordered. These aircraft were Braniff's first four-engine airliners, and delivery began on November 6, 1945. On May 5, 1946, DC-4 service was inaugurated between San Antonio and Chicago. Braniff employed 1,500 and operated 21 aircraft. (BFC/HAC.)

At the end of 1945, Braniff inaugurated cargo service on all routes, using Douglas C-47s. The magnificent Douglas DC-6 was just around the corner for Braniff, and new routes to the Southern Hemisphere would highlight 1946. (BFC/HAC.)

Braniff executive vice president Charles Beard, above, is given a special bouquet of flags that represented the nine nations served under the company's new Latin America route authority. Beard was departing on a special survey flight of the region on August 25, 1946. The company was awarded the 7,719-mile route system between the United States and Latin America on May 22, 1946. The new routes made it necessary to acquire larger airliners such as the Douglas DC-6 Skyliner shown below painted in the 1950 color scheme. The company ordered six additional DC-6s and five DC-4s on June 25, 1946. By the end of 1946, Braniff inaugurated the first nonstop flights from Dallas to Chicago Midway with DC-4s and employed 2,533. (Both, BFC/HAC.)

Two

Ho! Down
South We Go

Braniff Airways officially became an international air carrier when it inaugurated service to Latin America on June 4, 1948. A sleek Douglas DC-6 flew the first passengers from Dallas to Houston and then south to Havana, Cuba; Panama/Balboa City, Panama; and Guayaquil, Ecuador, where it arrived early the following morning. Over the next five years, the airline inaugurated the remainder of the 7,719-mile Latin route system.

In August 1952, Braniff merged with Kansas City–based Mid-Continent Airlines (MCA), which further enlarged Braniff's route system. MCA operated a fleet of Douglas DC-3 aircraft and had the new 42-passenger Convair 340 twin-engine aircraft on order.

The year 1953 was one of reflection for Braniff, as the carrier was burdened by its South America system, which had not made money. The merger with MCA also placed strains on the Braniff's financial portfolio, mainly as a result of postal rates paid on MCA's airmail contracts. The combination of these two problems caused Braniff to record a substantial operating loss, which was offset by the sale of new aircraft.

Problems did not end in 1953; and in January 1954, the company patriarch, Tom Braniff, was killed in a private plane crash in Louisiana. With the company since 1935, executive vice president Charles Beard, with a heavy heart, took the reins of Braniff and within one year returned the company to profitability. Tom's son, Thurmon, had died in a plane crash in 1937 and his daughter, Jeanne, died in 1948 of complications from childbirth. New aircraft were ordered, including the long-range Douglas DC-7C airliner, dubbed El Dorado, propjet-powered Lockheed Electras, and the company's first pure jet aircraft, the Boeing 707.

Legend.

Domestic and International Routes of
BRANIFF INTERNATIONAL AIRWAYS

Proposed extensions of
BRANIFF INTERNATIONAL AIRWAYS

Connecting Air Service

With the Latin America award, Braniff officially changed its trade name to Braniff International Airways and began touting its new routes on timetables and this route map from the 1947 annual report. A special preinaugural flight departed on February 5, 1947, with Thomas Elmer Braniff and Besse "Bess" Clark Thurmon Braniff and guests on board. The DC-4 flight traveled to 11 countries and was the first four-engine plane to fly over the Latin routes. In April 1947, Braniff became the first certificated to use an instrument landing system (ILS) to guide its planes to landings on inclement weather days. The system featured vertical as well as horizontal guidance to the runway. Braniff introduced instant confirmation of air and hotel reservations on May 1, 1947. (BFC/HAC.)

The magnificent Douglas DC-6 Skyliner was delivered to Dallas on August 25, 1947, and entered scheduled service on November 5, 1947. Featuring a pressurized cabin and a cruising speed of 300 miles per hour, the airliner was placed in service between Texas and Chicago. The cabin interiors were designed by Jeanne Braniff and equipped with berths on South American flights. Ship N90883 is pictured here at Dallas Love Field in 1947. (BFC/HAC.)

Service to South America was near, and on May 22, 1948, a 13-day preinaugural flight was flown with a DC-6 from Dallas and Houston to Cuba, Panama, Ecuador, Peru, and Bolivia. On June 4, 1948, the first scheduled flight departed Dallas Love Field for Houston, Panama, and Guayaquil, Ecuador. This Braniff Douglas DC-6 is parked at Limatambo Airport, Peru, in 1949. (BFC/HAC.)

Service to Latin America was quickly expanded, with Lima, Peru, added on June 18, 1948, using DC-4 and DC-6 aircraft. The first coach service ever was offered on DC-4 flights. Braniff flew its one billionth passenger mile of accident-free operation on August 30, 1948, and international parcel service was begun in September. During 1949, service was added to La Paz, Bolivia, and Rio de Janeiro, Brazil. (BFC/HAC.)

Once a week, Braniff operated a DC-4 to Latin America that offered both freight and passenger service. Dubbed the Tourist Liner, it featured leather passenger seats fitted with the backs at the window, facing each other, and offered similar comfort to regular flights but with a lower fare. Two hostesses wearing Western-style uniforms served a barbecue dinner while en route. The unidentified hostess is assisting Pat Zahrt of Braniff public relations. (BFC/HAC.)

Braniff became the first carrier certified to use jet-assisted takeoff (JATO) on its DC-4 aircraft operating from high-altitude La Paz El Alto Airport, Bolivia, on January 17, 1949. Captain Carleton headed the test group and is second from right with JATO dischargers and DC-4 N65145. Scheduled service began with DC-3s at La Paz on February 8, 1949, and on June 3 of that year, the first scheduled service using JATO began. (BFC/HAC.)

Braniff began service between Lima and Rio on March 9, 1949, and at 2,548 miles, it was the longest nonstop in the world. In September, Braniff dubbed its Latin America–bound DC-6 aircraft El Conquistador and the DC-4 El Intercontinental, denoting the levels of service. Full first class was offered on El Conquistador, while lower fares were offered on El Intercontinental flights. In 1950, service was expanded to Buenos Aires and then to São Paulo in 1951. (BFC/HAC.)

Braniff ordered 20 new Convair 340 twin airliners for $12 million on March 5, 1951. On August 16, 1952, Kansas City–based Mid-Continent Airlines was merged into the Braniff system. MCA operated in the Midwest with 23 DC-3s and four Convair 240s over 6,241 route miles serving 35 cities. The company operated 10-passenger Lockheed Lodestars from 1940 until 1945, such as Ship NC25602. (BFC/HAC.)

A new Braniff Convair 340-32 N3406 is parked at Des Moines Airport, Iowa, in 1953. Braniff became the first airline to inaugurate service with the 44-passenger plane on November 1, 1952, from Dallas Love Field. Each Convair cost $600,000, and they became the last piston propellers remaining in Braniff's fleet before being retired in 1967. (BFC/HAC.)

By 1953, Braniff had grown to a major domestic and international carrier and celebrated its 25th year of service. However, the merger with MCA and the Latin America expansion had proved costly, resulting in a loss for 1953, which was offset by the sale of new Convair 340 aircraft. The company's fortunes would change in 1954, with a modification of mail subsidy it was paid over the former MCA routes. (BFC/HAC.)

During 1953, Braniff retired its DC-4s and inaugurated DC-6 combination cargo/passenger flights to Latin America and the first coach service between Dallas and Chicago with Convair 340s. (BFC/HAC.)

Sleeper berths were inaugurated on the first DC-6 flights to South America in June 1948, offering a full range of amenities, including push-button release, makeup kits, thermos containers, reading lights, and call buttons for only $25 extra. The service was extended to domestic service beginning on March 1, 1950, between Dallas and Chicago. (BFC/HAC.)

After a less-than-stellar financial year exacerbated by a strike of maintenance employees, Braniff was shaken to its core on January 10, 1954, when Tom Braniff (second from right in this 1942 photograph) was killed in a private plane crash near Shreveport, Louisiana. Braniff's brother Paul (second from left) died of bone cancer in June, and Bess Braniff (right), Tom's wife, died in August 1954. (BFC/HAC.)

Pictured here is Braniff's magnificent operations and maintenance base at Dallas Love Field in 1952. The massive Lockheed hangars that Braniff began occupying in May 1946 are in the foreground. Three additional hangars were leased in 1950, which brought the number of buildings to 21, with 300,000 square feet of space on 66 acres. (BFC/HAC.)

On April 5, 1954, Braniff had flown three billion passenger miles on a flight between Dallas and Chicago and received its 21st safety award in June for an accident-free 1953. Braniff and Eastern inaugurated interchange service between Newark, Washington, DC, and Miami to Latin America with DC-6s on August 18, 1955. (BFC/HAC.)

Braniff began the first DC-6 flights to Latin America equipped with airborne weather radar on April 15, 1954. The company was the best trunk line carrier during 1954 for completion of scheduled domestic flights. A remarkable 98.96 percent of 21,799,378 plane miles were completed. (BFC/HAC.)

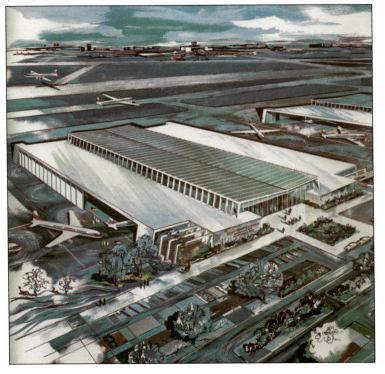

In an agreement signed with the City of Dallas on June 10, 1955, Braniff pledged to build a $6 million, 36-acre maintenance and operations base. A ground-breaking ceremony was held on June 20, 1956, Braniff's 38th anniversary. Designed by Pereira and Luckman Architects, two Mid-century modern hangars were planned, but only one was constructed, at 7701 Lemmon Avenue. (BFC/HAC.)

Additional capacity was needed on domestic routes, and two used Lockheed L-049 Constellations from Linea Aeropostal Venezolana (LAV) of Venezuela were added to the fleet in 1955 (right). The Constellations carried 54 at a speed of 290 miles per hour and were only in the fleet until 1959. To supplement its cargo business, Braniff added two Curtiss C-47 Commando twin-engine planes (below) to its fleet in December 1955. (Both, BFC/HAC.)

On March 17, 1955, Braniff announced the purchase of seven Douglas DC-7C four-engine long-range airliners for $20 million. The DC-7Cs were dubbed El Dorado after the famed city of gold in Colombia. They cruised at 360 miles per hour and carried 74 passengers over distances of 5,000 miles. Also during 1955, $87 million was approved for new piston, jet-powered, and jet aircraft. (BFC/HAC.)

The first DC-7C was delivered to Dallas on September 13, 1956, and flown from California by Capt. R.V. Carleton. Service began between Texas and Chicago, Newark, and Washington, DC, on October 20, 1956. Archbishop Robert E. Lucy (left) and Msgr. Bernard F. Popp bless the new airliner. (BFC/HAC.)

DC-7C El Dorado service was inaugurated to Latin America in May 1957 along with the introduction of Gold Service on international routes. Silver Service, offered on domestic routes, was begun on the Dallas-to-Newark inaugural, February 11, 1956. Both in-flight experiences featured beverages served with silver sets and offered the finest in-flight cuisine. (BFC/HAC.)

A new graduating class of Braniff hostesses pose for a 1957 group photograph. The hostesses are wearing the 1957 two-piece summer uniform in powder blue. The following year, hostess Terry Labus would create a new winter uniform made of all-wool gray flannel. She won a contest for best uniform. (BFC/HAC.)

On April 7, 1957, Braniff moved its corporate office from the Roanoke Drive "Red Brick Building" to Exchange Bank Tower at Exchange Park near Love Field. The move was temporary until the new 10-story Braniff Tower was complete. Braniff moved into it on Valentine's Day 1958. Braniff's largest shareholder and director, Sen. William A. Blakley, developed the Exchange Park Complex. (BFC/HAC.)

Pictured here is the handsome entrance doors to the 10th floor executive offices at Braniff's new Exchange Park tower. Charles Beard's and other executives' offices were housed on the 10th floor, which featured unique outdoor terrace gardens for each office. The University of Texas Southwestern now owns the Exchange Park complex and beautifully maintains Braniff Tower today. (BFC/HAC.)

On January 7, 1956, Braniff ordered five new Convair 440 Metropolitan twins for $4 million. The new aircraft seated 44 passengers and featured a quieter exhaust. They entered service on domestic routes on December 10, 1956, and remained in service until 1966. Ship N3437 is parked at Fort Worth Greater Southwest Airport in September 1960 and was the only one with the sleek radar dome. (BFC/HAC.)

By the end of 1957, Braniff carried more than two million over 37 million revenue passenger miles. On its 30th anniversary, June 15, 1958, Braniff's fleet numbered 68, carrying 5,000 passengers each day. Braniff moved into its spectacular new 415,000-square-foot Operations and Maintenance Base on the east side of Love Field on October 4, 1959. (BFC/HAC.)

Braniff ordered nine jet-powered Lockheed L-188 Electra four-engine aircraft on December 14, 1955. The total cost for the planes was $22 million, and they carried 75 in mixed configuration at a speed of 405 miles per hour. Braniff's second Electra N9702C is being prepared for its 13-foot diameter propeller installation at Lockheed's Burbank, California, plant. (BFC/HAC.)

Ship N9701C was delivered at the Lockheed Burbank Plant on March 20, 1956. Captain Carleton flew the first Electra back home to the Dallas Love Field base. The second Electra, Ship N9702C, is shown on the South Hangar ramp at the Dallas Base after being flown from Burbank to Dallas on May 7, 1959. The Electra remained in service until April 1969. (BFC/HAC.)

The new Electras were placed in service between San Antonio, Dallas, and Newark and Houston, Dallas, and Chicago Midway on June 15, 1959. The elegant interiors of the Electra were designed by Henry Dreyfuss, designer of the famed Western Electric Model 500, 302, Princess, and Trimline telephones for AT&T. (BFC/HAC.)

Braniff entered the jet age on December 1, 1955, when President Beard ordered five Boeing 707-227 Intercontinental Jets. The new four-engine pure jets were bought for use on long-haul domestic and international routes and could cruise at 600 miles per hour carrying 112 passengers. Braniff's first 707-227 N7071 is shown parked at the Boeing Renton, Washington, plant in October 1959. This aircraft was lost during a demonstration flight at Oso, Washington, on October 19, 1959. (BFC/HAC.)

In January 1959, Braniff's new operations and maintenance base, above, hosted an open house for employees and the public to become acquainted with the new facility. This 1960 photograph was taken above Lemmon Avenue with a view looking west and the former Lemmon Avenue Terminal visible in the upper left corner closest to the taxiway. In May 2013, the base was deemed by the National Park Service to be eligible for listing in the National Register of Historic Places and is in the process of being restored. Below, Braniff's magnificent new Boeing 707-227 El Dorado Super Jet was the company's first pure-jet aircraft. The Love Field base was specifically built to handle these new aircraft with special tail cutouts placed above Bays 3 and 4 of the North and South Hangars. (Both, BFC/HAC.)

Three

Those Magnificent Jets, Charles

Braniff recorded its greatest growth period to date between 1954 and 1964, under the guidance of the company's new president Charles E. Beard, who ascended to the chief position after the death of company cofounder Tom Braniff on January 10, 1954. The company achieved record increases in revenues and traffic each of those years, as it officially entered the jet age.

President Beard ordered the company's first jet airliner, the Boeing 707, as well as Lockheed L-188 Electra jet-powered airliners. These magnificent new planes began delivery to Braniff in the summer of 1959 and officially ushered in the jet age at the Dallas-based carrier. New routes were awarded to the East Coast, and the new Boeing 707s and Electras were perfectly suited for these longer routes.

The new jets enabled Braniff to increase its capacity, and as a result the company reported record earnings between 1954 and 1964. Revenues more than doubled from $45 million in 1954 to $109 million in 1964, which also marked the first time in company history that revenues exceeded $100 million. After 30 years, Beard announced his desire to retire in November 1964, on the eve of the arrival of Braniff's first twinjet short-haul airliner, the BAC One-11.

Braniff's first jet-powered aircraft, the Lockheed L-188 Electra, was placed in service between Dallas and Washington, DC. The first nonstop scheduled service between Houston and Chicago was inaugurated on October 1 with Electras, and service was extended from Dallas to Amarillo, Colorado Springs (pictured here on inaugural day with chamber of commerce and military guests), and Denver on November 16. (BFC/HAC.)

Braniff entered the jet age on December 3, 1959, when its first Boeing 707-227 arrived at the Dallas base. The new super jet flew from Boeing's Renton, Washington, plant at a remarkable 602 miles per hour and recorded flight time of only two hours and 52 minutes. Passengers on the 707 were given a special Jet Speed Record Club souvenir certificate to commemorate their trip. (BFC/HAC.)

The Boeing Super Jet entered service on December 19, 1959, acting as Santa's Super Jet, Ship N7072, carrying toys from Dallas to New York for needy children. From left to right on the ramp are Pres. Charles Beard, Vice Pres. Rex Brack, and executive vice president J.W. Miller and his wife, on hand for the inaugural at Love Field. The next day, a second Santa's Super Jet flight was made from Dallas to Chicago Midway. (BFC/HAC.)

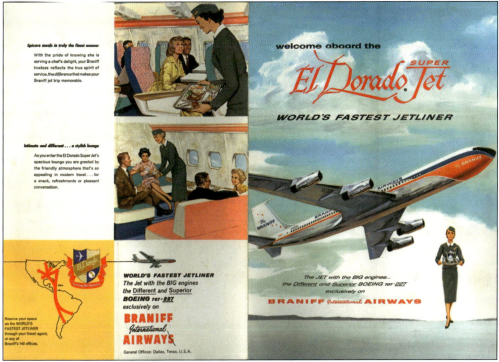

A special full-color brochure was created to introduce Braniff's new jet. Braniff's 707s featured a standard 707-120 series fuselage with more powerful 320 series engines. And fast they were—on a flight from Dallas to New York on January 5, 1960, a record was made of two hours and seven minutes of flight time at 685 miles per hour. Braniff touted the 707 as the "Jet with the Big Engines" and the "World's Fastest Jetliner." (BFC/HAC.)

A master of economy, Braniff built its own tug bar at the Dallas base, saving thousands. Foreman D.R. Robertson (left) and tow designer Bob McCord are testing the new tool in September 1959. (BFC/HAC.)

With the advancement to jets, Braniff was in need of new hostesses to man the cabins. Hostess Terry Labus is featured on the front of this 1960 brochure announcing the Hostess Career Program. Qualifications required the applicant to be single, which remained company and union policy until hostess Betty Green Bateman challenged it in court in 1965 and won, setting a new industry precedent. In 1969, hostess Jill Parker Snow challenged the company's maternity policy and also won. (BFC/HAC.)

Braniff's renowned Silver Service was unmatched in the industry, and on board the new 707, it made every flight memorable. Elegant and luxurious interiors were designed by Gale Authors and featured four-abreast seating in first class and six-abreast in tourist. Hostesses are wearing the Chanel-inspired jet jacket uniform that debuted on the December 19, 1959, inaugural of the 707. (BFC/HAC.)

Braniff invaded Latin America with Boeing 707-227 jet service on January 22, 1960, when a special preinaugural flight flew 50 guests from the publishing, civic, and business communities on a flight that covered 15,158 miles in 32 hours and two minutes flying time. Scheduled service began on April 1, 1960, with service to Panama, Lima, and Buenos Aires. Bogota, Colombia, received its first jet service with 707s from the United States on July 18, 1960. (BFC/HAC.)

Braniff ordered Boeing 720-027 jets on March 10, 1960. The order for six of the medium-range four-engine jets was placed with Boeing, with delivery scheduled to begin in February 1961. Made from newer lightweight materials but similar in appearance to the 707, the aircraft seated 106 passengers. Ship N7079 is parked at the gate at Dallas Love Field in 1962. (BFC/HAC.)

Hostess Terry Labus Wilcox is modeling the 1962 summer hostess uniform in front of the new Boeing 720-027 in 1962. This was the last uniform before the introduction of the Emilio Pucci Gemini IV Collection in July 1965. In 1957, Braniff held a contest for hostesses to submit a new design for a winter uniform, and Wilcox won with her sharp two-piece gray flannel ensemble. (BFC/HAC.)

On May 20, 1961, Braniff purchased a new Boeing jet simulator, which was installed at the Dallas base. The simulator featured a replica of the front section of the aircraft coupled with electronic equipment that allowed for the simulation of flight. The jet simulator, built by Link Aviation and installed on August 17, 1961, afforded Braniff the luxury of reducing actual aircraft training hours. (BFC/HAC.)

Braniff's route system was growing steadily by September 1962. New Boeing jet service was expanded to São Paulo and Rio de Janeiro in 1960, and on November 9, 1960, it inaugurated Electra service between Minneapolis/ St. Paul, Minnesota, and Mexico City. The new service was the first since the Mexican government pulled Aerovias Braniff's operating certificates in 1946. (BFC/HAC.)

Passengers traveling from the continental United States to Latin America aboard the Boeing 707 Super Jet are enjoying Braniff's impressive Gold Service. The hostess, wearing her new jet jacket uniform, is serving appetizers and beverages from a gold serving set. On July 22, 1960, Braniff welcomed its 20 millionth passenger on a flight from Dallas to Houston. (BFC/HAC.)

On December 1, 1960, Braniff inaugurated the only nonstop Douglas DC-6A all-cargo service between Dallas Love Field and Newark Airport. Ship N90776 is being prepared for the inaugural flight on the south ramp at the Dallas Love Field base. (BFC/HAC.)

Sen. William A. Blakley, Braniff's largest shareholder, resigned from the board and sold his Braniff stock and that of the Blakley/Braniff Foundation to a group of Texas Instruments founders. Braniff's new largest shareholders included J. Erik Jonsson (later mayor of Dallas), Eugene McDermott, Patrick Hagerty, and Cecil Green. A Braniff Douglas DC-6 El Conquistador is parked at the Dallas base in 1950. (BFC/HAC.)

Braniff began looking for a replacement for its Convair and Douglas DC-6 aircraft in the early 1960s, and the British Aircraft Corporation (BAC) One-11 Fastback Twinjet was chosen. Six of the short-to-medium-range jets were purchased along with options for six additional units for $35 million. Braniff's first BAC One-11 Ship N1541 is pictured here during a 1964 test flight. (BFC/HAC.)

Important new service was added during 1962, including an interchange with Pan Am that operated from Houston to Frankfurt, Germany, via Dallas, Chicago, and London, that began on July 1. A new terminal was opened at New York Idlewild on November 18, and the new Dulles Airport opened the next day, with the inauguration of nonstop jet service from Dallas. Revenues for 1962 were $84 million, a record, with profits of $2.4 million, up 90 percent over 1961. (BFC/HAC.)

Braniff offered Pan Am $22 million for Panagra on April 29, 1963, and the following day announced that its planes flew 100 million revenue passenger miles in a single month over the domestic system for the first time in its history. On June 20, the company celebrated its 35th anniversary by announcing it had flown 12.5 billion revenue passenger miles, carrying 27 million passengers over 490 million miles. The plush first-class lounge was the place for fine service on Braniff's Boeing 707-227s. (BFC/HAC.)

The jet age was ushered in quickly at Braniff, with Boeing jets flying throughout the United States and Latin America by 1964. On October 31, 1963, a new record was set when 99.4 percent of domestic flights were on time. Record revenues of $98 million highlighted 1963 along with 88.1 percent of 119,215 flights operating on time. (BFC/HAC.)

Braniff president Charles Beard (left) and BAC One-11 designer Sir George Freeman Edwards are viewing "The New Jet" during a visit to Hurn, England, in 1963. Additional orders were placed for the new twinjet during 1963 and 1964, bringing Braniff's total order to 14. (BFC/HAC.)

Braniff vice president of operations R.V. Carleton chaired the first Supersonic Transport Conference in Montréal, Canada, on April 17, 1961. The outcome of this conference was Braniff's placement of deposits on two delivery spots for a US supersonic transport (US SST) for the early 1970s. Three manufacturers submitted designs, but the magnificent Boeing 2707 was the winner. Congress canceled the program in 1970. (BFC/HAC.)

The Blakley/Braniff Foundation dispersed $30 million of its assets to charities, including the University of Dallas, on May 20, 1964. An endowment of $7.5 million was given, with $1.5 million used to build the Braniff Graduate Center, Braniff Mall, and Tom and Bess Braniff Memorial Tower, and the remainder of the funds placed in an endowment for the university. The Braniff Center, designed with a Latin American theme, was the work of O'Neil Ford of San Antonio, Texas. (BFC/HAC.)

Braniff celebrated its 36th anniversary with the announcement that it had flown 29 million passengers over a distance of 525 million miles, equaling 13.5 billion revenue passenger miles, since it first began service on June 20, 1928. A Braniff DC-6, Ship N90884, is being loaded with airmail in 1950. The aircraft is painted in the 1950 red-and-blue color scheme, which was modified with the addition of a white upper fuselage in 1951. (BFC/HAC.)

Braniff Airways, Inc., would be changing dramatically—and soon. (BFC/HAC.)

Insurance magnate Troy Victor Post (left) purchased Braniff on July 8, 1964, when his Greatamerica Corporation obtained 51 percent of Braniff's outstanding shares. The shares were owned by a group of Texas Instruments executives who had purchased them from the Blakley/Braniff Foundation in 1961. Braniff lit up like a star in New York's Time Square (below) when a massive sign became part of the city's nightlife on July 24, 1964. The sign was believed to be the largest moving message sign in existence at that time. (Both, BFC/HAC.)

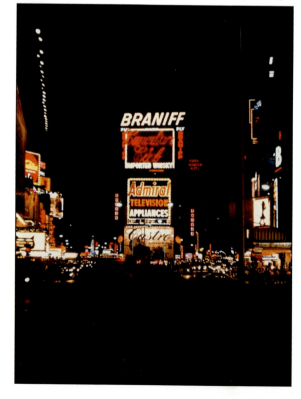

Four

IF HARDING SAYS WE CAN DO IT

In 1964, Braniff Airways, Inc., was sold to insurance magnate Troy Victor Post and his Greatmerica Corporation. Post intended to fly Braniff to magnificent new heights in regards to the product it provided. He enlisted a young Continental Airlines executive, Harding Luther Lawrence, to help him achieve his lofty goal. Lawrence, a native of Perkins, Oklahoma, and a Texas transplant, was perfectly suited to create a new world-class Braniff and assumed the presidency on April 5, 1965.

Braniff's new president entered his new position with intensity and enlisted the help of a Madison Avenue advertising firm to assist him in creating the new Braniff. Jack Tinker and partners Mary Wells, Stu Rich, and Dick Greene designed the revolutionary End of the Plain Plane campaign, which called for bold new aircraft paint schemes and designer employee uniforms—a complete departure from the staid military styles that had been the hallmarks of airline images since their founding.

The End of the Plain Plane campaign was a smashing success, with traffic increasing virtually overnight while Braniff's stock price skyrocketed. Spectacular new jets were ordered while Braniff's revenues increased in one year the same amount that it had taken the company to realize since its founding in 1928. Braniff became the airline that everyone wanted to fly, to own, and to work for; it was the toast of the town, and the new employee watchword was "If Harding says we can do it, we can!"

In November 1964, Pres. Charles Beard announced his intention to retire after 30 years of exemplary service. During his tenure as president, Braniff had grown from $41 million in revenues in 1953 to $109 million in 1964. Troy Post announced on February 10, 1965, that 44-year-old Continental Airlines executive vice president Harding Luther Lawrence was chosen as Beard's successor. (BFC/HAC.)

One-11 Jet became the new buzzword at Braniff on March 13, 1965, with the arrival of its first new BAC One-11 Twinjet. Later, it was dubbed the Fastback Jet after styling that was prominent in automobile design at the time. The first One-11, Ship N1543, was flown from the Hurn plant to Newark, New Jersey, where it was delivered and then flown to Love Field. (BFC/HAC.)

The New York advertising firm Jack Tinker and Partners was hired on March 26, 1965, and on April 5, Harding Lawrence assumed the presidency of Braniff while Ed Acker became senior vice president of planning. Braniff officially became known as Braniff International on April 19, 1965. A Braniff Boeing 720 and two Electra jets are parked at the gate at Dallas Love Field in 1962. (BFC/HAC.)

Lawrence announced the largest order for new aircraft in Braniff's history on May 3, 1965. The $118-million order included five Boeing 707-327C long-range jets and 12 Boeing 727QC trijets. A mix of Braniff jets painted in the new solid color scheme at the gate at Love Field is pictured here in 1966. (BFC/HAC.)

Mary Wells of Jack Tinker and Partners created the basic idea for the new End of the Plain Plane look, which revolutionized how the company's aircraft and facilities appeared to the public. New Mexico architect Alexander Girard was tasked with creating the new look. Girard redesigned 17,543 public contact and corporate items for Braniff, including a new solid color scheme, such as lemon yellow on this Boeing 720 at Love Field in late 1965. (BFC/HAC.)

Eight colors were chosen by Girard for Braniff's jet aircraft, including turquoise, lemon yellow, beige, periwinkle blue, dark blue, pale blue, ochre, and orange. Seven new interior color designs were created in red, blue, grey, yellow, brown, green, and orange. Here, Girard (seated) is in his New Mexico studio designing the new Braniff look, including this new logo, in June 1965. (BFC/HAC.)

Haute couturier Emilio Pucci created a new wardrobe for Braniff's employees, including flight and ground personnel. The new fashions, dubbed Gemini IV, featured a whimsical array of unique fabrics and designs inspired by the Project Gemini spaceflight missions. Hostess uniforms included an outfit for each segment of the flight, while a unique Air Strip was performed to introduce each garment. (BFC/HAC.)

In July 1965, a Boeing 720 N7076 was painted in periwinkle blue and used for a photo shoot at Love Field for a *Life* magazine advertisement. It was determined that the purplish hue was not culturally acceptable in Mexico and Latin America, and it was discontinued. A special blue filter was used in the advertisement, and the Boeing was repainted in dark blue the following month. (BFC/HAC.)

The periwinkle blue Boeing 720-027 N7076 is taxiing at Dallas Love Field in the summer of 1965. The color and the black script were symbols of death and sorrow in Mexico. The harmless black witch moth, believed to be a harbinger of death in Mexico, bears purple markings. Pink, green, and brown were also initially chosen, but were only used in advertising. (BFC/HAC.)

Braniff's new look was unveiled to the world on November 6, 1965, during a special ceremony at the Dallas base. Two Boeing 720s and two BAC One-11s made a flyby and then landed and taxied to the ramp for a closer inspection and interior tour. The Boeing 720-027 N7076 in periwinkle blue was repainted in dark blue before taking part in the ceremony. (BFC/HAC.)

By the end of 1965, a battalion of colorful jetliners, like these at the Love Field Yellow Concourse, was flying throughout the Braniff system. The *Life* magazine advertisement debuted on Christmas Eve, and a week later Braniff ended its most profitable year in history, with revenues of $129 million and earnings of $9.4 million, up 58 percent over 1964. (BFC/HAC.)

Braniff's new drive-in and baggage check-in facility at the Love Field base on Lemmon Avenue is under construction on April 29, 1966. Passengers could buy tickets and check their luggage at the first automated ticket facility of its kind. On June 4, 1966, movie actress and Dallas resident Dorothy Malone was the first to use the new facility. (BFC/HAC.)

On April 21, 1966, Braniff ordered nine new jets, including four Boeing 727s, four 727QCs, and one 707-327C, at a cost of $53 million, with delivery beginning in January 1967. Boeing 727-27C N7272 is painted in the 1965 Girard pale sky blue solid color scheme in this predelivery photograph in 1966. (BFC/HAC.)

That same month, Braniff founded the Board of International Chefs, tasked with creating an in-flight menu featuring the finest in culinary delights. Executive chef Willy O. Rossel, who arrived from the Sheraton Hotel in Dallas, headed a group of renowned chefs from North and South America. Chef Rossel is pictured here ensuring his signature dessert is perfectly prepared. The Braniff hostess is modeling the new Pucci Supersonic Derby uniform, which debuted on June 27, 1966. (BFC/HAC.)

Braniff International welcomed its first Boeing 727-162 N7282 at the Love Field base on May 12, 1966. Originally ordered by Pacific Northern Airlines, N7282 was initially painted dark brown at the Boeing factory but was changed to turquoise. Because N7282 was taken first, it arrived before Braniff's first ordered 727-27C N7270, which arrived later, on May 27, 1966. (BFC/HAC.)

On May 27, 1966, Braniff took delivery of its first Boeing 707-327C convertible passenger/cargo four-engine long-range jet. The majority of these jets were assigned to the PAC-MAC charters, which began on June 2, 1966, from Travis Air Force Base in California, to Honolulu Hickam and the Far East. Lemon-yellow ship N7096 is taxiing at Love Field on delivery day, May 28, 1966. (BFC/HAC.)

During the summer of 1965, Braniff retired its Douglas DC-6 fleet. However, three aircraft were painted in Alexander Girard test colors, including this DC-6, above and below, which was painted dark blue on one side and red on the other. Two other DC-6s were painted in solid colors and sold to an airline in Peru, but none in that color scheme ever entered service with Braniff. (Both, BFC/HAC.)

On July 5, 1966, Braniff began military charters from Charleston AFB, South Carolina, to Puerto Rico and the Canal Zone and from McGuire AFB, New Jersey, to Newfoundland, Greenland, and Iceland. A month later, on August 1, 1966, Braniff inaugurated the world's first nighttime 727 quick-change cargo service between San Antonio, Dallas, and Chicago. Quick-change seating is being removed from a 727QC for a nighttime cargo flight from Love Field in 1967. (BFC/HAC.)

A Braniff Boeing 707-327C flew the first nonstop flight from Tokyo, Japan, to Love Field on September 15, 1966. The flight was returning from a PAC-MAC charter and flew the route in 10 hours and 58 minutes. On December 1, 1966, Braniff retired its last Douglas DC-7C, which had served since 1956. (BFC/HAC.)

The company reported its most profitable year in history with a net profit of $17.8 million, an increase of 88 percent over 1965. Braniff also hired the New York industrial design firm Harper and George to freshen the original solid colors. The striking red on this 727-27 N7293 was one of seven new, or updated, colors. (BFC/HAC.)

On February 1, 1967, Braniff merged with Pan American Grace Airways (Panagra), making Braniff the largest US carrier flying between the United States and Latin America. Panagra operated Douglas DC-8 four-engine aircraft and also had five DC-8-62 long-range jets on order. Panagra's proposed color scheme for the Series 62s was only painted on this model. Braniff paid $30 million for Panagra, and the deposits Panagra had paid on the DC-8-62s were worth $27 million—making it a fantastic deal. (BFC/HAC.)

New service in 1967 included a Pan Am interchange flight from California to Chile; the first nonstops Dallas to Seattle and Portland; the first express through plane service from Oklahoma City to Washington, DC; Dallas nonstop to Corpus Christi, Texas; and nonstop service from Miami to Quito, Ecuador. Braniff introduced the Council Club in 1965, which offered access to members-only lounges designed by Alexander Girard. (BFC/HAC.)

Braniff opened a new fully automated cargo facility at the south end of Love Field on July 6, 1967. Braniff's new cargo facility was the largest fully automated cargo facility in the United States. The new Jetrail, a people mover that opened in 1970, shadows Braniff's colorful new cargo center at Tom Braniff Drive and Aviation Place. (BFC/HAC.)

The magnificent new Douglas DC-8-62 entered service between the United States and South America on September 4, 1967. The new jet could carry 156 passengers over a distance of 6,500 miles. Braniff's Douglas DC-8-62 N1804 is flying high in the new Harper and George two-tone blue color scheme, which was introduced in November 1971. On September 5, 1967, the last Convair was retired, making Braniff a completely jet-powered airline. (BFC/HAC.)

Pictured here is the impressive Braniff ticket office in the lobby of the Adolphus Hotel in downtown Dallas. The classic Girard designs continued to be used in all areas of Braniff until a new look was adopted in 1971. (BFC/HAC.)

Besides the original eight solid colors designed by Girard, there was also this green featured on a one-fifteenth-scale Boeing 707-227 model by Westway of England. This model was displayed at the Love Field base for the November 6, 1965, debut of the new look and flyby. The pilot is wearing the 1965 Pucci Gemini IV black gabardine uniform. (BFC/HAC.)

Hostess Sue Pedler Golden is modeling the classic Pucci 1966 Supersonic Derby Collection from high atop a Boeing 720 wing. Golden is wearing the purple uniform, but it was also available in pink. (BFC/HAC.)

Braniff opened its new five-story Hostess College at 2801 Wycliff Avenue, north of downtown Dallas. The $2-million facility was dedicated on January 5, 1968. Designed by Dallas architect firm Pierce Lacey and associate architects John Allen Pierce, Neal Lacey, and Jim Henderson, the five-story facility could house 142 Braniff hostesses in training. (BFC/HAC.)

Interior design of the hostess college was by Chuck Ax of Florida and featured classic Girard elements throughout the building. Each dorm room had twin beds and brilliant color accented with Girard's Arts and Crafts look. Braniff occupied the building until 1975. (BFC/HAC.)

Fashion designer Emilio Pucci introduced his third collection for Braniff, dubbed the Classic Collection, on May 28, 1968, at the Plaza Hotel in New York. The fashions were simplified and featured two colorways of pale pink and plum. Hats were discontinued and replaced with colorful Pucci Vivara scarves, and hair could be worn long for the first time if in a bun or chignon. (BFC/HAC.)

Braniff ended 1968 with profits of $10.4 million and revenues of $292.6 million compared to $256 million in 1967. On December 6, 1968, Braniff moved into its new Terminal of the Future at Dallas Love Field. The impressive terminal featured covered jetways for Braniff passengers for the first time at Love Field and the impressive rotunda pictured here. (BFC/HAC.)

The Terminal of the Future featured 11 new gates and two gates previously in operation. Each gate was decorated with elegant furnishings of Herman Miller furniture by Charles and Ray Eames and terrazzo floors. Braniff occupied the terminal until it moved to the new DFW Airport in January 1974. (BFC/HAC.)

On April 27, 1969, Braniff became an all-jet airline with the retirement of the Lockheed L-188 Electra II fleet. An Electra is being prepared for departure at Love Field's Yellow Concourse in 1962. Later that summer, long-fought-for service to Honolulu and Hilo, Hawaii, was inaugurated from Love Field on August 1, 1969, with Boeing 707-327Cs. (BFC/HAC.)

Revenues climbed to a historic $323.3 million, yielding $6.2 million in profits. The company was now three times larger than it was only five years earlier. In January 1968, Braniff chairman Harding Lawrence announced the purchase of two Boeing 747-127 Super Jets. Lawrence proudly displays two 747 models with Harper and George orange and green color schemes at his Exchange Park office. (BFC/HAC.)

On April 18, 1970, the Braniff Jetrail car park system went into service at Love Field. The monorail was the first of its kind installed at an airport for movement of passengers from remote parking to and from the terminal. Brightly painted air coaches whisked passengers above traffic delays. (BFC/HAC.)

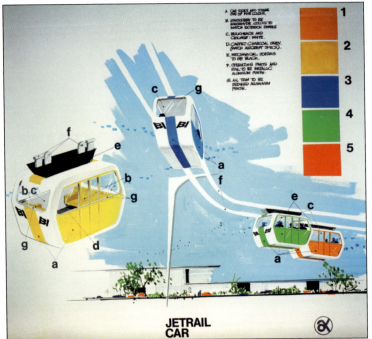

JETRAIL
CAR

The Stanray Corporation of Chicago, Illinois, designed the Jetrail system, and Dallas architect John Allen Pierce designed the lounges. Designer Chuck Ax created the color schemes and interiors of the lounges and air coach cars. His original design called for silver stanchions, but Federal Aviation Administration (FAA) obstruction regulations required that the stanchions be painted white with orange tracks. (BFC/HAC.)

Emilio Pucci returned on December 1, 1970, for the debut of his fourth line for the airline, dubbed 747 Braniff Place Pant Dress Collection. The new fashions featured a simple pant dress that could be worn with lounge pants and later matching hot pants. Made of Qiana fabric from DuPont, the garments were easy to wash and wear. Braniff hostesses model the pant dress at the Wycliff Hostess College boutique in 1971. (BFC/HAC.)

In summer 1969, Braniff purchased four used Boeing 707-138B long-range jets from Qantas Airways. In 1971, Braniff announced a new fleet-standardization plan that called for only Boeing 727, Douglas DC-8, and Boeing 747 aircraft; by 1973, the last of the Boeing 707 and BAC One-11 fleets were retired. Here, Boeing 707-138B N105BN is taxiing at Love Field in 1971. (BFC/HAC.)

On June 30, 1970, the first three Boeing 727-227 aircraft were delivered at the Love Field base. These jets, in addition to two leased Series 200s, were the last to be painted in the 1965–1967 Girard/Harper and George solid color scheme. Braniff ended 1970 with a $3-million loss, its first since 1953's operating loss. The nation had been hit with a recession, and three airlines were on strike. Braniff's mutual aid payments of $2.7 million accounted for the majority of the loss, which was the lowest loss of all the nation's airlines that year. (BFC/HAC.)

Braniff's first Boeing 747-127 N601BN, dubbed *747 Braniff Place* and nicknamed the *Great Pumpkin* by air-traffic controllers and later *Fat Albert* by Braniff employees, was delivered to the Love Field base on January 5, 1971. Ten days later, the jet assumed the daily nonstop from Dallas to Honolulu. However, the second Boeing 747-127 N602BN was traded for 727-200s. (BFC/HAC.)

The luxurious 747 first-class Blue Suite was the ultimate in airline furnishings. Designed by Harper and George with fabrics by Jack Lenor Larsen and seating, or chairs, by Jerry Okuda, each cabin was themed by color. The Green, Red, and Yellow Rooms housed coach-class passengers. An upstairs International Lounge contained additional lounge chairs. (BFC/HAC.)

Braniff returned to profitability in 1971, reporting an $8.6 million profit with record revenues of $332 million. New service was initiated, with nonstops between Love Field and La Guardia, Memphis, and Washington, DC; every hour on the hour between Dallas and San Antonio; Miami to Lima; and the first nonstops between Dallas and Newark, New Jersey. Braniff's new 747 quickly became the highest flight-time 747, flying seven days a week between Dallas and Hawaii. Harding Lawrence announced that the company would purchase 35 new Boeing 727-200s and also announced a new wide-body look for its narrow-bodied jets. Shrewdly, Braniff did not order large numbers of new jumbo jets such as Boeing 747s, Lockheed L-1011s, and Douglas DC-10s. Instead, it opted to provide frequency of schedule by offering several 727 flights for one jumbo jet flight offered by competitors. (BFC/HAC.)

On December 10, 1971, Braniff's first jet with the wide-body interior, dubbed *727 Braniff Place*, entered service. Four new two-tone color schemes also debuted along with new colorful interiors all designed by Harper and George. Emilio Pucci introduced his Blue Collection of hostess uniforms on June 15, 1972, pictured here with a 727 in blue over light blue. (BFC/HAC.)

In 1973, Braniff commissioned Alexander Calder, the master of kinetic art, to paint a Douglas DC-8-62 jet in a scheme to celebrate 25 years of Braniff service to Latin America. Dubbed *South America with Flying Colors*, the jet was revealed on October 29, 1973, soon after the dedication of the new DFW Regional Airport. The Calder DC-8 has just been rolled out of the Dallas base hangar after receiving its new paint scheme. (BFC/HAC.)

All airlines operating at Dallas Love Field, except Southwest and Braniff local Texas operations, moved to the new DFW Airport on January 13, 1974. In September 1973, a dedication ceremony was held where Braniff hosted the arrival of Concorde for the first time on US soil. (BFC/HAC.)

Emilio Pucci revealed his final collection for Braniff, Pucci Classic, on April 8, 1974. The basic elements of the new collection were a slim-tailored tunic, sweater, and body shirt, and slim trim-legged pants. A planned 1975 Flying Colors Pucci collection was planned but did not materialize. Pucci did design Flying Colors coveralls for maintenance personnel only. (BFC/HAC.)

The Braniff Terminal 2W at DFW Airport consisted of 18 departure lounges with dramatic and colorful entrances with BI-themed wall covering designed and produced by Wolf-Gordon. (BFC/HAC.)

Alexander Calder was commissioned again in 1975 to create a paint scheme to celebrate the United States' bicentennial celebration. The remarkable *Flying Colors of the United States* was painted on Boeing 727-291 N408BN, debuted on November 16, 1975, and was dedicated by First Lady Betty Ford the following day. Revenues for 1975 were $598.8 million, with profits of $16 million. (BFC/HAC.)

American haute couturier Roy Halston Frowick was commissioned by Braniff to create a completely new uniform that conformed to its new edict of elegance and sophistication. The Elegance campaign featured new Ultra solid paint schemes for Braniff's jets, leather seating on all aircraft, and the new Halston fashions, which debuted at the Three Evenings to Remember party in Acapulco, Mexico, on February 17, 1977. The Halston uniform and coach-class leather seating are shown. (BFC/HAC.)

On November 11, 1976, Alexander Calder was working on his third design for a Braniff jet, dubbed *Salute to Mexico*, to celebrate 15 years of service to the country. Calder died that evening, but the last model he was working on was chosen for the design, which was revealed at the Halston party in Acapulco. Pictured here is the *Salute to Mexico* Boeing 727-200 scale Westway model. The design was never painted on a Braniff jet because of the arrival of the new sleek Ultra color scheme in 1978, and because, with the death of the artist, it would not be an original work of art. (BFC/HAC.)

Pres. Jimmy Carter approved a long-coveted route between Dallas and London Gatwick on December 21, 1977. The daily nonstop 747 service marked the first time the southwestern United States and Europe would be directly connected. Above, Braniff offered daily cargo service between Texas and London, and a special orange truck moved freight between Gatwick and Heathrow Airports. On February 28, 1978, Braniff's Boeing 747-127 N601BN flew the inaugural flight from DFW Airport to Gatwick. A contingent of local guests was on board for the inaugural and toured London until their return on March 4, 1978. Below, agents at Braniff's bustling Gatwick ticket counter are handling DFW-bound check-ins for the return inaugural flight on March 4, 1978. (Both, BFC/HAC.)

Five

HOW MAGICAL
IT WILL BE

Braniff celebrated its golden anniversary in 1978, and the inauguration of new nonstop service from Dallas to London was the perfect complement to an extraordinary year. Braniff's first Boeing 747 assumed duty over the London route, while a leased 747 began the trek between Dallas and Honolulu, once again breaking operational records. Concorde service commenced in early 1979, which marked the first time a US airline had ever flown a supersonic transport in scheduled service.

Since the arrival of Harding Lawrence in 1965, Braniff had blossomed from $109 million a year to $900 million in revenues in only 13 years. The growth was unprecedented, and industry-leading profits were another gem in Braniff's impressive crown of accomplishments. Company financial records were broken in 1979, when the company surpassed $1 billion per year in revenue. By 1980, it had grown close to $1.5 billion.

In 1979, jet fuel prices rose by nearly 100 percent, and along with interest rates on the new jets topping 20 percent coupled with a general downturn in the economy in 1981, the great airline began to falter. Braniff became the first airline to file bankruptcy after deregulation, but it was far from being the last. The accomplishments of Braniff were impressive and its revolutionary change in how airlines presented themselves to customers would live on in honor of America's Most Colorful Airline.

Braniff operated only one Boeing 747-127 N601BN when the London award was granted, and it had been flying the DFW to Honolulu route. A second 747-123 N9666 was leased from American on January 11, 1978, to use on the Hawaii route, while N601BN assumed London service. N9666, departing DFW in 1978, was painted with an orange stripe and Girard BI tail logo. A new Boeing 747-227B was also purchased for delivery in May 1979. (BFC/HAC.)

Record earnings of $36.4 million on revenues of $791.2 million for 1977 were announced. Braniff petitioned the CAB for new service to the Middle East, and the CAB gave tentative approval for Concorde service. Colorful Braniff 727s are parked at the gate at DFW Airport in 1978. (BFC/HAC.)

On June 20, 1978, Braniff celebrated its 50th anniversary, having flown 90 billion revenue passenger miles during that time. A month later, on July 17, 1978, Braniff introduced its Ultra Color Scheme, which featured eight solid colors for its jet aircraft, including terra-cotta, light corvette blue, chocolate brown, Perseus green, Mercury blue, metallic blue, burgundy, and sparkling burgundy. Above, a Perseus green 727-2B7 N405BN is landing at DFW in 1979. Painted in the new Mercury blue color scheme, Boeing 727-227 N421BN is pictured below at DFW Airport on April 14, 1978. This was the first aircraft to receive the Mercury blue paint scheme. (Both, BFC/HAC.)

The finest in the air, Braniff's Halston-clad flight attendants pose for a photograph after serving Dallas-to-London passengers on the inaugural flight on February 28, 1978. The full Halston collection is visible in this photograph, which was taken aboard 747-127 N601BN in the Green Room. (BFC/HAC.)

Halston also designed durable fashions for Braniff's ground-service personnel. This crew has just unloaded a new Mercedes-Benz from the cargo hold of 747-127 N601BN at DFW after its arrival from London in March 1980. For winter weather, Halston designed a heavyweight padded overcoat in dark brown and a heavy-duty bright-yellow rain suit with brown Braniff Ultra script on the back. (BFC/HAC.)

In September 1978, Braniff petitioned the CAB for the following route authorities: Houston and DFW to Honolulu, Hong Kong, Guam, Okinawa, Manila, Taipei, Bangkok, Singapore, and Seoul; DFW and Boston; Cleveland and Pittsburgh; 747 service from Seattle and Portland to Honolulu; and in October, DFW and Boston to Paris and Frankfurt, Amsterdam, and Brussels. Pictured here is a Boeing 727-227 N435BN departing DFW in 1979. (BFC/HAC.)

On December 4, 1978, Braniff moved into its modern Mediterranean-style Braniff Place World Headquarters on the west side of DFW. Dubbed the "White Palace on the Prairie," the 446,000-square-foot complex featured four low-rise interconnected buildings with indoor-outdoor recreation facilities for employees. The $75 million facility allowed Braniff to consolidate all of its operations there, except for the major maintenance hangar at Love Field. (BFC/HAC.)

The impressive headquarters featured the flags of Braniff's global destinations. The parking area in front was lined with Italian tile in a striking Mediterranean blue. The second building featured a large cafeteria and data-processing, while the third building housed flight operations as well as the Braniff House Hotel. The fourth building featured recreation and conference rooms. Houston designer Sally Walsh conceived the colorful interior. Verizon now owns the Braniff Place World Headquarters building. (BFC/HAC.)

Braniff took full advantage of the Airline Deregulation Act. On December 15, 1978, the company inaugurated service to 16 new cities over 32 routes. It was the largest single-day expansion of any airline in the history of aviation. The Braniff Boeing 747 at DFW Airport dwarfs Braniff Boeing 727s in 1979. Braniff ended 1978 with record revenues of $972 million and net income of $45.2 million. (BFC/HAC.)

On January 12, 1979, two Concorde SST airliners line up simultaneously on the east and west runways at DFW Airport. The arrival of an Air France and British Airways Concorde marked the beginning of Braniff's new interchange service between Dallas and Washington Dulles and either London Heathrow or Paris Charles De Gaulle Airports. Braniff was the only US carrier to operate Concorde in scheduled service in the United States. (BFC/HAC.)

Braniff announced the $155.1 million purchase of three new Boeing 747 aircraft for its planned transatlantic and transpacific services on December 18, 1978. On May 31, 1979, Braniff took delivery of its first new 747 since 1971. Painted in the orange Ultra color scheme with International Ultra script, the striking Boeing 747-227B N602BN is parked at DFW in June 1979. (BFC/HAC.)

On June 1, 1979, Braniff embarked on its largest international expansion with the simultaneous inauguration of services from DFW Airport and Boston Logan to Paris, Frankfurt, Amsterdam, and Brussels. Inaugural ceremonies were held at both DFW and Boston. Three of Braniff's 747s arrived at the same time at DFW, officially marking the beginning of the new transatlantic services. (BFC/HAC.)

Braniff hostess Fran Claycomb Blanchard and Jack Witherspoon are enjoying the impressive Ultra Service cuisine in the first-class section of a new Boeing 747. The pair traveled to Paris, France, in August 1979 for a Braniff photographic assignment. Sumptuous leather seats were the hallmark of Braniff 747s. (BFC/HAC.)

Braniff inaugurated service across the Pacific beyond Honolulu on July 3, 1979. Boeing 747s operated the new route from Los Angeles to Honolulu, continuing to Guam and Hong Kong. Boeing 747SP-27, special-performance aircraft, were ordered for the new transpacific routes, with the first (N603BN) arriving from the Everett, Washington, plant on October 30, 1979. (BFC/HAC.)

Ship N603BN, Braniff's first long-range lower-density Boeing 747SP-27, is parked at Los Angeles International Airport in 1979. The new airplane seated 300 passengers and could fly 7,200 miles nonstop, making it perfect for the long transpacific flights from Los Angeles to Seoul, Korea, (Braniff's longest route) and Singapore. Braniff operated three 747SP aircraft beginning in 1979. (BFC/HAC.)

By 1980, Braniff operated a fleet of 108 modern jets, including 11 Boeing 727 Series 100s and 78 Series 200s, 10 Douglas DC-8-62s, six Boeing 747 Series 100s and 200s, and three Boeing 747SP-27s. Besides being the largest airline at DFW, it also operated the most Boeing 747s there as well. (BFC/HAC.)

By the end of 1980, Braniff's fortunes had reversed, along with the rest of the industry, as a result of intense competition from lower-cost carriers, unprecedented rises in fuel costs (from 38¢ in 1978 to $1.01 per gallon in 1981), a national recession, and credit card interest rates. These factors led to the cancellation of several new aircraft orders, including this Boeing 747-227B N605BN in flight over Washington State on June 10, 1980. (BFC/HAC.)

Above, a Braniff International Boeing 747 touches down at Dallas/Fort Worth Regional Airport in 1979. This jumbo jet is painted in the 1978 orange Ultra color scheme. From 1971 until 1982, Braniff either operated or had on order and then cancelled a total of 16 747s. At right, a Braniff Boeing 727 is taxiing at DFW in 1979 painted in the chocolate brown Ultra scheme with Braniff Ultra script. The 727 was the backbone of the Braniff fleet, and the airline had pressured Boeing to make a stretched Boeing 727-300. Although Braniff is not flying, its memory is carried on by the preservation efforts of Braniff Airways Foundation/Braniff Preservation Group, Preservation Dallas, Docomomo International, the University of Texas at Dallas, University of Dallas, UT Southwestern, and many others that are concerned with the legendary history of Braniff Airways. (Both, BFC/HAC.)

DISCOVER THOUSANDS OF LOCAL HISTORY BOOKS FEATURING MILLIONS OF VINTAGE IMAGES

Arcadia Publishing, the leading local history publisher in the United States, is committed to making history accessible and meaningful through publishing books that celebrate and preserve the heritage of America's people and places.

Find more books like this at
www.arcadiapublishing.com

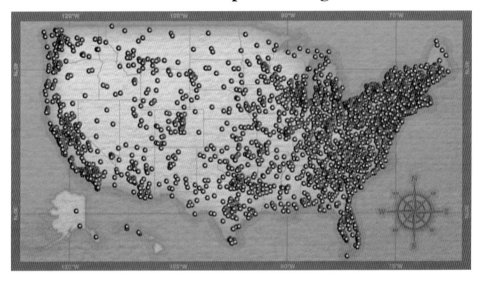

Search for your hometown history, your old stomping grounds, and even your favorite sports team.